D1723836

India at a Crossroads

Hindu Nationalist Efforts to Eradicate Christianity

Pieter Friedrich

— Dedication —

Gracious Father, Risen Son, Holy Spirit, we beg Thee to remember Thy Church belongs to Thee. We beseech Thee for the Christians of India to be refreshed by the fragrance of Thy sweet purity. May their wounds be blessed, their burdens be relieved, their oppressors be loved.

Holy Trinity, Thou knowest that the Deceiver, Destroyer & Prince of Darkness spreads his net over Thy Church in India so as to strangle Her. Have mercy on Her, O Lord. Comfort Her with the Truth that Thou hast trampled death by death. May She know the Enemy is already defeated.

Amen.

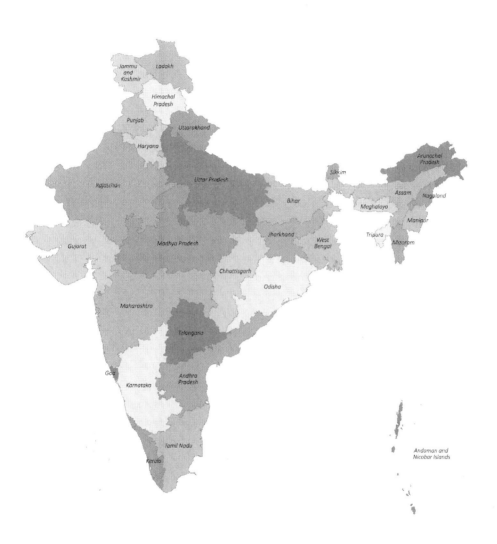

Map via VectorStock. Reprinted with permission.

— TABLE OF CONTENTS —

India's Increasingly Besieged Christians: Accused of Serving "Foreign Masters"

"I can hit you, don't worry," the woman tells a meek pastor as she slaps him in a video filmed in the central Indian state of Chhattisgarh in September 2021. "I can obviously hit you. Don't think that since police are standing [here that I can't]. If you try to argue, I will bloody smash you."

The pastor bows his head and thanks his attacker. She reaches up to choke him, pushing him against the hood of a police jeep. He smiles, silently. "If you show off in this sector, I will bury you here," she threatens as a police officer standing directly next to her watches passively. Touching his other cheek, the pastor says, "Hit me here also. You can do whatever you want."

Turning to the crowd gathered around her, the woman instructs them: "I am telling this to everyone. If they are seen anywhere, you have full permission from my side: hit them as hard as you can! Women or men, it doesn't matter, if you've come to put Hindutva [Hindu nationalism] in danger. First beat them, and then call me." Turning back to the pastor, she continues shouting, "Where do you live? Where do you live with your group? We need your full written address. Come to the police station, and wherever you live, you will vacate your houses."

"I am warning you, if you come here, you will see," threatens a saffron-robed Hindu swami standing on the other side of the police jeep. "Hail Mother India," he screams, as the crowd and even the pressured pastor join his chant. "Traitors of the country," he shrieks, and the mob finishes his sentence with "beat these bloody fellows."[1]

The casual acceptance of anti-Christian violence, the perspective that Christians are "traitors" who endanger the prevailing Hindu nationalist movement simply be existing in India, and the total dereliction of duty by police officers — all succinctly illustrated in this shocking two minute video — are no longer isolated incidents in India. They have become the new normal.

In November 2021, dozens of pastors in the southwestern state of Karnataka were contacted by police and instructed to stop holding prayer meetings because, they were warned, "police will not be able to give them protection." As *The Wire* reported, "Instead of going after those threatening law and order, the police have decided to ask Christians to lay low."[2]

The impotence of the police was again obvious in a September 2021 incident in Chhattisgarh. After police summoned a priest and two others to the station to question them about allegations of "forced religious conversions," a mob barged in and utter chaos erupted. Screaming "Hail Lord Ram," the mob began beating the Christians as police struggled to intervene. Just a week before, another priest was at home in a neighboring region when a mob of 100, angered that he had allegedly been converting people, invaded his house to beat him up.[3]

In a sense, however, as victims of non-State actors rather than the State itself, those priests fared bettered than two Christians who were arrested (also in September 2021) in the northern state of Uttar Pradesh for allegedly "carrying out forcible conversions." Police themselves beat the Christians in the station. One victim reports that officers accused them of eating "food from Indian soil" while serving "foreign masters," saying, "You are sharing about Jesus and attracting Hindus towards your faith. How dare you convert Hindus to Christianity?"

"My heart could sense that the officers would not let me go easily, and I was being reminded of verses from the Bible, and an inner voice was preparing me that I should not let fear consume," said Sabajeet, one of the brutalized victims. "I was recalling the verses in my heart and was being prepared for the humiliation and the physical pain I was subjected to later that night." Upon their release, they were threatened with prosecution if they refused to stop holding worship services. "Currently, we are praying secretly inside our homes, and the neighbors are looking for a chance to frame us in a false case of forced conversions," Sabajeet said. "It could be an overnight custody and beating without anybody knowing what is happening with us."[4]

With the exception of some horrific but mostly sporadic incidents over the past 25 years, Indian Christians have generally lived in peace and safety since India's independence in 1947. That began to change drastically when the Hindu nationalist Bharatiya Janata Party (BJP) rose to national power in 2014. Ever since, reports of rising persecution have steadily increased.

In 2021, the violence exploded. Yet many outside India — including, most shockingly, the international Christian community — remain largely ignorant of the gravity of the situation. In most cases, they seem totally unaware that there is even any problem whatsoever.

As violence increases, however, and India now ranks among the most dangerous countries in the world in which to be a Christian, concerns rise that the Hindu nationalist movement's ideological dedication to eliminating non-

Hindus — including Christians — from India is gaining such ground within the country that they may soon face an existential crisis.

Citations:

[1] Conversion Zindabad. Twitter Post. 7 October 2021. https://twitter.com/ConversionOK/status/1446113894678741006

[2] Prasanna, Pooja. "Belgavi: Cops Tell Christians to Skip Prayer Meets to Avoid Right-Wing Attacks." *The Wire.* 29 November 2021.

[3] "Chhattisgarh: Mob beats up Christian priest, two others inside police station in Raipur." *Scroll.* 6 September 2021.

[4] "Police Beat Christians in Custody in Uttar Pradesh, India." *Morning Star News.* 12 October 2021.

"Crackdown on Christianity": A "Hostile" Environment of "Extreme" Persecution

Christianity first arrived in the south of the Indian subcontinent when the Apostles Bartholomew and Thomas traveled there, according to tradition, within the first 20 years after the crucifixion of Jesus Christ. India today, with a population of 1.4 billion people, is home to approximately 30 million Christians — or more. American historian Dr. Philip Jenkins suggests that "a more realistic estimate of India's Christian population" would be 45 million, which, as he notes, "means that India has a larger Christian population than virtually any European nation."[1]

In 2013, India ranked 31st among the top 50 countries in the world where persecution of Christians is most severe, according to Open Doors USA. The nonprofit, which focuses on monitoring global persecution of Christians, categorized the situation in India at the time as one of "moderate persecution." By 2015, a year after the BJP came to power, India ranked #21; in 2016, #17; in 2017, #15; in 2018, #11.

By 2019, as BJP Prime Minister Narendra Modi was re-elected to a second term, India had joined the top ten countries where it's most dangerous to be a Christian; the persecution level was now categorized as "extreme."

As of 2022, India has now held the ignominious title of Tenth Most Dangerous Country for Christians for four years in a row. The level of persecution present ranks India higher even than many other countries more commonly associated with Christian persecution, including China, Saudi Arabia, and Sudan. However, Open Doors tracks persecution across multiple categories and so, if one were to consider persecution solely within the category of "violence," India, in the latest report, actually ranks among the *top six most violent countries* for Christians.[2]

Notably, while there are nine other countries where persecution of Christians, taken across all categories, does rank higher, India has three distinguishing factors from them all: first, it is the *only* legitimate, officially secular democracy on the list; second, as the second-most populated country in the world, its population is more than *twice* that of all the other nine combined; third, it is the *only* country which is an ally of the United States.

"The persecution of Christians in India is intensifying as Hindu extremists aim to cleanse the country of their presence and influence," reported Open Doors in January 2022. "The driving force behind this is Hindutva, an ideology that disregards Indian Christians and other religious minorities as true Indians because they have allegiances that lie outside India, and asserts the country should be purified of their presence. This is leading to a systemic, and often violent and carefully orchestrated, targeting of Christians and other religious minorities."[3]

Notably, among the top ten most dangerous countries in which to be a Christian, India is the *only* one in which Christians *and* Muslims *both* face persecution from the *same source*: militant Hindu nationalists.

"The main persecutors are well-organized Hindu extremist groups, local governments and nationalist Hindus who seek to 'purify' India by making it entirely Hindu," explained Voice of the Martyrs (VOM), a renowned nonprofit dedicated to defending the human rights of persecuted Christians, in its latest report. "They seek to appease Hindu deities by eliminating Christians, and they view Christian converts as traitors to the Hindu homeland." VOM, which labels the environment for Indian Christians as "hostile," further warns, "Hindu nationalist informants live in nearly every village and report on the activities of Christians, resulting in attacks and arrests."[4]

In November 2021, International Christian Concern (a US-based nonprofit which advocates for persecuted Christians) named India (along with six other countries) a "Persecutor of the Year," reporting: "Since Prime Minister Narendra Modi and his Bharatiya Janata Party (BJP) took power in 2014, Christian persecution has skyrocketed. Inspired by the notion of establishing India as a Hindu nation, Modi and the BJP have passed laws and enforced policies targeting Christians and limiting their religious freedom."[5]

In the nearly eight years since the Modi regime came to power, documented attacks on Indian Christians have increased by over four-fold. According to United Christian Forum for Human Rights (UCF), an India-based watchdog group, there were 127 anti-Christian attacks in 2014.

Every single year since then (but one) has seen those numbers ratcheting up, concluding with 505 reported attacks in 2021.[6] It was, stated UCF, the "most violent year" for Indian Christians.[7] In the words of Dr. John Dayal, a retired journalist and UCF co-founder, it was a "year of fear."[8]

"In almost all incidents reported across India, vigilante mobs composed of religious extremists have been seen to either barge into a prayer gathering or round up individuals that they believe are involved in forcible religious conversions," reported UCF in December 2021. The group further explained:

> "With impunity, such mobs criminally threaten, physically assault people in prayer, before handing them over to the police on allegations of forcible conversions. Often communal sloganeering is witnessed outside police stations, where the police stand as mute spectators. Sadly, this violence against the Christian community is compounded by the failure of police to investigate and prosecute mobs and perpetrators."[9]

Over 300 of those attacks were recorded in just the first nine months of 2021; most significantly, approximately 95 percent of those were mob attacks in which sometimes as many as hundreds of people invaded Christian churches and even homes.[10]

The majority of these attacks occurred in states with so-called "anti-conversion" laws — particularly Uttar Pradesh, Chhattisgarh, Karnataka, and Jharkhand. These laws essentially criminalize the freedom of religious conversion. Provisions vary, but they typically require that, when someone wants to convert, either they or the clergy involved in the conversion ceremony — or both — must inform (and sometimes even receive permission from) the local magistrate and undergo a waiting period of, in some cases, up to two months. Failure to do so is punishable by hefty fines as well as prison sentences ranging, in some states, up to as long as ten years.

Nine of India's 28 states currently have anti-conversion laws. Six of these states (Gujarat, Himachal Pradesh, Jharkhand, Madhya Pradesh, Uttarakhand, and Uttar

Pradesh), all while under BJP rule, passed or updated their laws only after the party gained national power in 2014. Another BJP-ruled state, Karnataka, is in process of passing a law. At least two other BJP-ruled states (Haryana and Assam) are actively considering such legislation.

"The laws ostensibly punish forced or fraudulent religious conversions," explains the Evangelical Fellowship of India (EFI). "But in practice, they are used to criminalize all conversions, especially in non-urban settings."[11]

Most ominously, ever since 2014, the BJP has regularly floated rumors that it will pass a national law criminalizing conversion. However, according to Dayal: "The presumption is that there is [already] an anti-conversion law across the country. Apart from these nine or ten states, in the other twenty states also, it exists also *ipso facto*. If not *de jure*, if not lawfully, then in the mind of the policeman, in the mind of the Hindu extremist, it exists."[12]

These laws embolden vigilante groups to enact violence against the Christian minority, something which has played out, most recently, in Karnataka.

"What makes the Karnataka anti-conversion law quite sinister is that its introduction in the legislature is running in parallel with a series of targeted attacks on churches, Christian prayers and Christmas celebrations," reported *The Hindu* in December 2021. "Belligerent right-wing groups are out in the field with what appears to be an agenda to create an impression that religious conversion is rampant and that urgent legislative action is necessary to stop the trend."[13]

People's Union for Civil Liberties (PUCL), an Indian human rights organization, warns that local police in Karnataka are often "seen colluding with the Hindutva supremacists to incite fear and hatred against Christians, and police commonly turn a blind eye to incidents of violence, abuse, sexual assaults, economic and social boycott." PUCL continues: "In some cases, large mobs barged in during Sunday morning prayer meetings, and executed violent attacks leading to injury, damage to property, psychological and physical trauma. In some others, smaller mobs disrupted prayer meetings, threatening murder, criminal charges of forced conversion, excommunication or even the revoking of reservation rights [affirmative action for historically marginalized castes]."[14]

Following many attacks, Christians were forced to shutter their places of worship, meaning the violence alone "act[s] as a bar on the freedom to practice religion itself."[15] State complicity is a central component. "In many cases of mob violence, the police arrested pastors and believers," reports PUCL. "They even issued formal notices to churches to stop prayer meetings."[16]

In Karnataka, violence escalated in anticipation of passage of the law; in many other states which have already passed such laws, vigilantes feel similarly empowered to commit violence with impunity because of the perceived legal cover provided by claiming that they are attacking those who are supposedly engage in "illegal" conversions.

Simply put, in the words of *The New York Times*, "laws against religious conversions have been accompanied by mob violence." Such violence is "propelled by a growing anti-Christian hysteria that is spreading across this vast nation, home to one of Asia's oldest and largest Christian communities, with more than 30 million adherents." As the paper's front-page headline stated in its 27 December 2021 issue, India faces a "crackdown on Christianity."

"Anti-Christian vigilantes are sweeping through villages, storming churches, burning Christian literature, attacking schools and assaulting worshipers," reported the *Times*. "In many cases, the police and members of India's governing party are helping them, government documents and dozens of interviews revealed. In church after church, the very act of worship has become dangerous despite constitutional protections for freedom of religion. To many Hindu extremists, the attacks are justified — a means of preventing religious conversions. To them, the possibility that some Indians, even a relatively small number, would reject Hinduism for Christianity is a threat to their dream of turning India into a pure Hindu nation. Many Christians have become so frightened that they try to pass as Hindu to protect themselves."[17]

Even as far back as 1999, Human Rights Watch (HRW) had already begun taking notice of mounting anti-Christian violence in India. "India's inter-religious violence now extends to Christians, and its underlying causes are the same as those promoting violence against Muslims, Dalits ('untouchables'), and other marginalized groups in the country — political and economic power struggles linked rhetorically to the creation of a Hindu nation," warned HRW.[18] They concluded that the groups most responsible for organized violence against Christians were then — as it remains now — the Rashtriya Swayamsevak Sangh (RSS) paramilitary and its offshoots.

"The RSS fuels a religiously intolerant narrative that views all non-Indic faiths, like Christianity and Islam, as foreign and something to be feared," explained Open Doors in 2021. "The RSS demonizes Christians and other religious minorities through these hateful narratives, instigating violence in the streets. The RSS also uses these narratives to advocate for laws and policies that are discriminatory against religious minorities.... Members meet daily and dedicate part of their meetings to martial arts training. Many members eventually use this training against religious minorities."[19]

Considering that the RSS views non-Hindus as second-class citizens, at best, and, in particular, views Indian Christians — and Muslims — as "traitors" who are "foreign" to the nation and, therefore, constitute "internal threats," its militant orientation, combined with its ideological outlook, naturally creates a deadly environment for religious minorities who, on multiple occasions, have already fallen beneath the paramilitary's proverbial sword.

Before examining the prior history of attacks on Indian Christians, which is relevant to understanding the gravity of the current situation, it's necessary to delve into the ideology of the RSS itself in order to comprehend why they are so antagonistic towards religious minorities.

Citations:

[1] Jenkins, Philip. "Has Christianity really failed in India?" *Union of Catholic Asian News*. 8 May 2015.

[2] Open Doors USA. "World Watch List." 2013 and 2015-2022.

[3] Open Doors USA. "World Watch List 2022." India profile.

[4] Voice of the Martyrs. "Global Prayer Guide 2022." India profile.

[5] International Christian Concern. "Persecutor of the Year Awards 2021." 29.

[6] David, Supriti. "Christians are 'target practice' for communal groups, say community leaders." *Newslaundry.* 28 January 2022.

[7] "2021 was 'most violent year for Christians in India': UCF report." *Sabrang India*. 31 December 2021.

[8] Dayal, John. Personal interview. 8 January 2022.

[9] Siddique, Iram. "Amidst BJP tribal push, Christian schools, churches feel the heat in MP." *The Indian Express*. 15 December 2021.

[10] Pal, Sumedha. "Over 300 Instances of Violence Against Christians Were Reported in Nine Months of 2021: Report." *The Wire*. 21 October 2021.

[11] Kaur, Surinder. "Indian Christians Discuss Different Reports on Persecution." *Christianity Today*. 19 August 2021.

[12] Dayal. Personal Interview.

[13] "Act of faith: On Karnataka anti-conversion law." *The Hindu*. 27 December 2021.

[14] "Criminalising the Practice of Faith." People's Union for Civil Liberties, Karnataka. December 2021. 9.

[15] Ibid. 10.

[16] Ibid. 20.

[17] Gettleman, Jeffrey and Suhasini Raj. "Arrests, Beatings and Secret Prayers: Inside the Persecution of India's Christians." *The New York Times*. 23 December 2021.

[18] Narula, Smita. "Politics By Other Means: Attacks Against Christians in India." September 1999.

[19] Open Doors USA. "Persecutor."

"Traitors": Why Hindu Nationalists View Indian Christians as "Internal Threats"

In his 1966 book, MS Golwalkar — the longest-serving and most influential Chief of the RSS, who is today revered as the paramilitary's "guru" — asked: "What is the attitude of those people who have been converted to Islam or Christianity?" Answering his own question, he claimed:

"They are born in this land, no doubt. But are they true to their salt? Are they grateful to this land which has brought them up? Do they feel that they are the children of this land and its tradition, and that to serve it is their great good fortune? Do they feel it a duty to serve her? No! Together with the change in their faith, gone is the spirit of love and devotion for the nation.... So we see that it is not merely a case of change of faith, but a change even in national identity. What else is it, if not treason, to join the camp of the enemy leaving their mother-nation in the lurch?"[1]

Simply put, Indian Christians — and Muslims — are, in the eyes of the RSS, traitors.

The RSS — whose name stands for "National Volunteer Corps" — was founded in the then British-occupied Indian subcontinent (in 1925) with a mission to "organize the entire Hindu society" and "put in reality" that "this is a nation of Hindu people."

The particularly menacing nature of the call to "organize the entire Hindu society" must not be overlooked. For the RSS's founders, their new paramilitary could not simply serve as *a* organization *within* the sphere of the Hindu religion, but must become the *sole* custodian of Hinduism, a head dictating and controlling the actions of *every segment* of the religion. This vision is explicitly stated by the RSS today, which openly says that it wants to "expand so extensively" that everything related to the religion will be "engulfed into its system."[2]

The paramilitary's five co-founders included the brother of VD Savarkar, a writer who published the book *Hindutva* (in 1923) to articulate the religious nationalist political ideology which he believed must undergird Indian polity.

"Hindutva," meaning "Hinduness," claims that the core identity of India is just that: Hinduness. Anyone in India who is not a Hindu is therefore, in essence, not considered a true Indian. Thus, non-Hindu Indians are consequently viewed as incapable of real patriotism.

Hindutva and its commitment to establishing India as a Hindu nation for — *and only for* — Hindu people is the foundational and governing ideology of the RSS. It's an ideology which, as phrased by the US Commission on International Religious Freedom (USCIRF), "holds non-Hindus as foreign to India."[3] It is also an ideology which originated not only alongside the rise of European fascism in the 1920s-1940s, but actually took inspiration from those very same fascists, praised their genocidal goals, and even directly interacted with them to some extent.

Soon after the Nazi party was formed in Germany (in 1920) and fascism took root in Italy (in 1921), Savarkar formulated his concept of "Hindutva" in India.

He argued that Hindus were not just a religious unit but also a "race" — one holding the only unique birthright to the land. "India must be a Hindu land, reserved for the Hindus," he wrote. "If you call it an Indian Nation it is merely an English synonym for the Hindu Nation. To us Hindus, Hindustan [Land of the Hindus] and India mean one and the same thing. We are Indians because we are Hindus and vice versa."[4]

Savarkar suggested that Christians and Muslims cannot exist as loyal Indian citizens because, unlike Hindus, they do not view India as *both* their "Fatherland" *and* their "Holy Land." As he argued:

> "For though Hindustan to them is Fatherland as to any other Hindu, yet it is not to them a Holy Land too. Their Holy Land is far off in Arabia or Palestine. Their mythology and Godmen, ideas, and heroes are not the children of this soil. Consequently their names and their outlook smack of a foreign origin. Their love is divided."[5]

He contrasted the allegedly suspect loyalties of Indian Muslims and Christians with those of Hindus, claiming, "Hindustan being their Fatherland as well as their Holy Land, the love they bear to Hindustan is undivided and absolute." He insisted that the way to keep "Hindustan" exclusively for Hindus was to form "a Hindu Nationalist Front," to "be prepared to fight any non-Hindu power that stands in the way of our onward march," and to "capture the political power that even today obtains by voting only for Hindu Nationalists." Doing otherwise, he claimed, was "to commit a cultural and political and racial suicide."

Ultimately, his clarion call was to "Hinduize all politics and militarize Hindudom."

In 1925, five adherents of Hindutva ideology joined together to form the RSS to, essentially, incarnate Savarkar's call for a militarized Hindu nationalist front. It was the same year that, in Germany, Adolf Hitler published *Mein Kampf* and founded the Schutzstaffel (SS); the Nazi concept that "blood and soil" defined nationality did not escape these RSS co-founders.

"We do not say that others should not live here," declared the first RSS chief, KB Hedgewar. "But they should be aware that they are living in Hindustan of Hindus." He repeatedly compared his concept to that of a "Germany of Germans."[6]

By 1931, RSS co-founder BS Moonje — who was Hedgewar's mentor — was reaching out to the European fascists to learn about their ideology and methodology.

During a ten-day tour of Italy, he visited the fascist youth groups and then concluded his trip by personally meeting Benito Mussolini. "The idea of Fascism vividly brings out the conception of unity amongst people," he wrote after his tour. "India and particularly Hindu India need some such Institution for the military regeneration of the Hindus.... Our Institution of Rashtriya Swayamsevak Sangh of Nagpur under Dr. Hedgewar is of this kind."[7]

Returning to India, Moonje reported seeing "with my own eyes" the "youth movement of Germany" and "Fascist organizations of Italy," stating: "They are eminently suited for introduction in India." In 1934, in a recorded conversation with Hedgewar, he insisted that India ought to also adopt the cult of personality implemented by the European fascists. Demanding "standardization of Hinduism throughout India," he declared:

"This ideal can not be brought to effect unless we have our own *swaraj* [independence] with a Hindu as a Dictator like... Mussolini or Hitler of the present day in Italy and Germany. But this does not mean that we have to sit with folded hands until some such dictator arises in India. We should formulate a scientific scheme and carry on propaganda for it."[8]

By 1940, Golwalkar — who would become the "guru" of the RSS and, in his 1960s writings, explicitly detail his idea that Indian Christians and Muslims are "traitors" — replaced Hedgewar as chief of the growing paramilitary.

In his 1939 manifesto, Golwalkar had echoed and expanded the Hindu nationalist admiration for Europe's fascists. Pointing to both Hitler's Germany and Mussolini's Italy, he praised their "race consciousness" and "race spirit,"[9] comparing it to the spirit and consciousness which the RSS sought to rouse and awaken so that the world would "see the might of the regenerated Hindu Nation strike down the enemy's hosts with its mighty arm."[10] Both fascist nations had proven, he argued, that "every race" possesses "the indisputable right of excommunicating from its Nationality all those who, having been of the Nation, for ends of their own, turned traitors and entertained aspirations contravening or differing from those of the National Race as a whole."[11]

This "indisputable right" of national excommunication included, in his mind, the right to demand that "foreign races" in India — that is, non-Hindus — agree to either "merge themselves in the national race and adopt its culture, or to live at its mercy so long as the national race may allow them to do so and to quit the country at the sweet will of the national race." Detailing what "merging" with the "national race" required, he wrote,

> "The foreign races in Hindustan must either adopt the Hindu culture and language, must learn to respect and hold in reverence Hindu religion, must entertain no idea[s] but those of the glorification of the Hindu race and culture, i.e., of the Hindu nation, and must lose their separate existence to merge in the Hindu race or may stay in the country, wholly subordinated to the Hindu Nation, claiming nothing, deserving no privileges, far less any preferential treatment — not even citizen's rights. There is, at least should be, no other course for them to adopt."[12]

This approach to minorities, he argued, was justified by the example of Nazi Germany. Noting how "German race pride has now become the topic of the day," he declared:

> "To keep up the purity of the Race and its culture, Germany shocked the world by her purging the country of the Semitic Races — the Jews. Race pride at its highest has been manifested here. Germany has also shown how well-nigh impossible it is for Races and cultures, having differences going to the root, to be assimilated into one united whole, a good lesson for us in Hindustan to learn and profit by."[13]

In Golwalkar's mind, in India, these different "races and cultures" who were ostensibly incapable of "being assimilated into one united whole" were, primarily, the

Christians and Muslims whom he accused of, by virtue of converting away from Hinduism, losing "their spirit of love and devotion for the nation," changing their "national identity," and engaging in "treason" by joining "the camp of the enemy."[14]

Particularly in his later writings in the 1960s, Golwalkar viciously accused Indian Christians and Muslims of adopting a "foreign mental complexion" by leaving the "Hindu fold." He insisted that "history does not record a single notable instance" of any Indian converting to Islam or Christianity out of sincere conviction. Their very existence as Indians following such faiths represented, he argued, "foreign domination," and required that they be called out of "religious slavery" back to "the ancestral ways of devotion and national life." After all, he claimed, the *only way* to achieve unity amongst all Indian citizens was "to fuse them all in the Hindu way of life."[15]

Failing to address this problem was supposedly an issue of national security. The presence of both Islam and Christianity in India constituted, in Golwalkar's words, "internal threats."[16] In fact, he even went so far as to claim that Christians and Muslims were conspiring to "join together and, between themselves, partition the country."[17]

Positing that Indian Muslims are universally secessionist, he argued that they treated every mosque in the country as "their own independent territory."[18] Even those serving in Indian government positions were, in his mind, "rabidly anti-national" figures whose "speeches carry the ring of open defiance and rebellion."[19]

Arguing that, "in practically every place," Indian Muslims maintained secret communications with Pakistan, he warned that they "are trying to undermine our very national existence."[20]

Christians, he insisted, are also "separatist" forces who are fundamentally "anti-national" and solely devoted to destroying the "nationalism" of Indian citizens.[21] The goal of Christians "residing in our land today" was, he said, "to demolish not only the religious and social fabric of our life but also to establish political domination." Indian Christians, he claimed, "refuse to offer their first loyalty to the land of their birth," behaving instead as "agents of the international movement for the spread of Christianity."

Declaring that, "wherever they have gone," Christians have been nothing but "blood-suckers," he concluded: "They will remain here as hostiles and will have to be treated as such."[22]

Such a prejudiced outlook would be disturbing enough in the average powerless hate-monger. Yet these weren't the mindless ramblings of a cranky, drunk old uncle shouting at passersby from his back porch. It was the ideological perspective of a man who served as chief of the RSS from 1940 until his death in 1973 — a man who is, today, revered as the paramilitary's Guru.

While little has changed about the RSS's ideology, everything has changed in terms of its modern-day access to social and political power.

Today, the RSS has an estimated six million direct members — notably, a number that *only includes* members who participate in *daily* activities. It has dozens of special purpose subsidiaries, but the most important and prominent of these are the Vishwa Hindu Parishad (VHP, which serves as a religious wing) and the Bajrang Dal (which serves as the VHP's youth wing). The VHP has (according to past estimates) nearly seven million members while the Bajrang Dal has (according to recent estimates) around five million members. Exact membership details are impossible to come by because none of these groups release figures, but, combined, they easily constitute a force surpassing 10-15 million or more.

The BJP, which serves as the political wing of the RSS, has perhaps 180 million or more members, making it the largest political party in the world. While not all BJP members are actively involved in the RSS or its subsidiaries, members of those groups control the BJP. "There is no difference between the BJP and RSS," a Hindutva activist once said. "BJP is the body. RSS is the soul."[23] Or, as a former US ambassador to India explained, "The RSS can survive without the BJP but the BJP cannot exist without the RSS."[24]

All of these — the RSS, VHP, Bajrang Dal, BJP, and other affiliates — are collectively known as "the Sangh Parivar" (Family of Organizations) or simply "the Sangh."

Current RSS Chief Mohan Bhagwat plans for the paramilitary to "reach every household" and establish branches in "all villages" of India by 2025.[25] Meanwhile, the RSS has already reached the highest halls of national power. Prime Minister Modi is an RSS member. So is President Venkaiah Naidu. So is Home Minister Amit Shah (who is in charge of the country's internal law and order). At last count, in 2019, 71 percent of Modi's current cabinet ministers have a background in the RSS (or one of its affiliates), up from 62 percent during his first term.[26]

The RSS has *de facto* ruled India since 2014. Its power is only growing stronger. The threat that poses for the future of Indian Muslims and, increasingly, for Christians, cannot be overstated.

This is not the first time that the BJP has held national power, however. Its first iteration as a national government (albeit a less powerful one as, within India's parliamentary system, it was then only a coalition government) was in 1998. It had a devastating impact on Indian Christians.

Comprehending how, today, the hateful teaching that Christians are "traitors" to India is translated into violence on the streets — violence which could spiral out of control at any time — requires first examining ways in which that has already happened in yesteryear.

Citations:

[1] Golwalkar, MS. *Bunch of Thoughts*. Bangalore: Vikrama Prakashan. 1966. 127-128.

[2] Rashtriya Swayamsevak Sangh. "Vision and Mission." RSS.org.

[3] United States Commission on International Religious Freedom. "Annual Report: India Chapter." 2010. 242.

[4] Savarkar, VD. *Hindu Rashtra Darshan*. Bombay: Syt. Laxman Ganesh Khare. 1949.

[5] Savarkar, VD. *Hindutva*. Bombay: Veer Savarkar Prakashan. 1923. 113.

[6] Apoorvanand. "He Came, He Spoke, the RSS Conquered." *The Wire*. 8 June 2018.

[7] Casolari, Marzia. *In the Shadow of the Swastika*. London: Routledge. 42.

[8] Ibid. 46.

[9] Golwalkar, MS. *We or Our Nationhood Defined*. Nagpur: Bharat Publications. 1939. 82-83.

[10] Ibid. 52.

[11] Ibid. 83.

[12] Ibid. 104-105.

[13] Ibid. 87-88.

14 Golwalkar. *Bunchs*. 127-128.

15 Ibid. 130-131.

16 Ibid. 166.

17 Ibid. 185.

18 Ibid. 174.

19 Ibid. 178.

20 Ibid. 176.

21 Ibid. 182.

22 Ibid. 185-186.

23 Human Rights Watch. "Anti-Christian Violence on the Rise in India."
30 September 1999.

24 Ambassador David Mulford. "The Bharatiya Janata Party: A House
in Disarray." Wikileaks. Wikileaks cable: 07NEWDELHI3031_a.

25 "RSS should reach every household in centenary year, says Mohan
Bhagwat." *The Hindu*. 11 September 2021.

26 Pandey, Neelam and Shanker Arnimesh. "RSS in Modi govt in
numbers — 3 of 4 ministers are rooted in the Sangh." *ThePrint*. 27
January 2020.

4

Burned for Christ: Hindu Nationalist Attacks on Christians Before the Modi Era

"Until recently, Christians enjoyed a relatively peaceful coexistence with their majority Hindu neighbors," reported HRW in 1999. "In the past several years, however, Christians have become the target of a campaign of violence and propaganda orchestrated by Hindu nationalist groups attempting to stem the tide of defecting low-caste and tribal voters."

The sea change began when the BJP first attained national power in 1998; one of the first major waves of violence occurred in the western state of Gujarat as the BJP also came to power there. Beginning on Christmas Day, 1998, Sangh organizations in the Dangs district of Gujarat spent ten days attacking Christian homes and churches, vandalizing or simply incinerating dozens. The violence, according to HRW, appeared "carefully organized by the leadership of extremist Hindu groups." Police were of little use in preventing — or prosecuting — the attacks:

> "Local police have not provided adequate protection to villagers in the affected areas, even though there have been early warnings of violence. In some cases, police have refused to register complaints by members of the Christian community, whereas they have registered complaints by others against Christians. Some Christians who have filed charges

with the police have been pressured to withdraw their complaints. Officers who have taken action in response to anti-Christian attacks have been threatened with transfers."

The embers of the arsonists in Gujarat were still warm when, in the eastern state of Odisha, another fire was kindled.

Australian missionary Graham Staines arrived in Odisha in the 1960s and soon dedicated his life to serving those afflicted by leprosy. While there, he met and married Gladys, fathered three children, and translated the Bible into a local tribal language.

In January 1999, Staines and his two sons — aged nine and six — were traveling overnight when they pulled over to sleep in their station wagon during what would be their final night on earth. "Over one hundred people reportedly poured petroleum on the station wagon and set it on fire," reported HRW. "As the family tried to escape, the mob held them back while shouting pro-Bajrang Dal slogans and physically assaulted villagers who tried to come to their rescue."[1]

Staines and his sons were burned alive.

The day of their death, police noted that the attack "was most likely perpetrated by the Bajrang Dal, an arm of the Rashtriya Swayamsevak Sangh."[2] That was soon confirmed with the arrest — and ultimate conviction — of the ringleader, a Bajrang Dal member who was also known as a local BJP activist. Before his apprehension, the killer continued translating Hindu nationalist ideology into on-the-ground violence; that year, he led gangs which burned alive a Muslim man and killed a Catholic priest with an arrow shot.[3]

The Staines murder drew international attention and outrage. However, as American professor of religion Dr. Chad Bauman notes, "Less recognized both by foreign politicians and in international press coverage was that Staines's death came just after anti-Christian riots in the Dangs, Gujarat, and in the midst of a period of heightened violence against Odisha's and India's Christians more generally." Within less than two months of the Staines murder, the Sangh was again setting fires.

"After a visiting BJP politician inflamed inter-religious tensions in Odisha by encouraging local Hindus to paint a trishul over a cross the Christians had erected on a hill nearby, rioters there set 157 Christian homes ablaze and attacked twelve Christians, leaving three of them with gunshot wounds," explains Bauman.[4]

"Since the end of 1998, Christians in India have been subjected to a wave of violence — bibles burned, churches looted, priests killed and nuns raped," reported *The New York Times* in November 1999. "The United Christian Forum for Human Rights says there were 38 recorded incidents between 1964 and 1996. In the last two years, there have been more than 150."[5]

The number of reported incidents continued to rise in 2000 and onwards, but when the BJP lost national power in 2004, the pattern of rapidly increasing attacks generally dropped off — with one extreme exception.

Anti-Christian sentiment in Odisha had been festering for years, and the state soon became a hotbed for the Sangh's campaign of hate. According to HRW: "In March 2002, VHP and Bajrang Dal activists, ostensibly annoyed at criticism from some legislators, attacked the state's Assembly; in February 2004, seven Christian women were beaten up and tonsured... to forcibly reconvert them to

Hinduism; and in August 2004, Hindu extremists stormed a church in Raikia town, burnt Bibles, and destroyed church property. One group, claiming inspiration from the RSS, even claimed it was setting up Hindu suicide-bomb squads."

Notably, since 2000, Odisha's state government was controlled by a regional political party allied with the BJP.

In 2005, this series of attacks inspired a coalition of human rights activists, attorneys, professors, and retired judges to form a people's tribunal to investigate the rise of sectarian violence. Seeking open dialogue with the RSS and affiliated groups, they invited them to join. A few activists agreed; leadership from some of the Sangh groups, however, denounced the tribunal, showed up to intimidate participants with threats of rape and other violence, forced the tribunal to destroy its recordings of depositions of Sangh activists, accused them of "attempting to destabilize the country," and compelled them to vacate the venue. Such an outcome led HRW to — prophetically — warn that year that "there is no time to wait" as the environment of hate being cultivated in Odisha meant that it only needed "a spark" to "lead to waves of violence that engulf whole communities."[6]

That spark was struck in December 2007, igniting a flame that then became a conflagration in August 2008.

On Christmas Eve, 2007, a group of Hindu nationalist activists (allegedly led by a local RSS leader) began to "rough up" Christians at a market in Odisha's Kandhamal district. Conflict between the two groups ensued. The Hindu nationalist mob swelled into hundreds and began attacking Christians and their shops. Shortly after, the convoy of a prominent VHP leader — a swami known for "openly campaigning against missionaries and working to reconvert Dalits and Adivasis [tribals] who had adopted Christianity"[7] — was stopped en route to the market, his bodyguards allegedly "roughed up some Christians," and a group of Christians responded by briefly surrounding and attacking his vehicle. By that afternoon and over the next several days, mobs of hundreds and even thousands of Hindu nationalists began rampaging throughout the district, burning Christian homes and churches, chanting: "Kill the Christians, destroy the church."[8]

By the end of it all, around 95 churches and over 600 Christian homes were razed. "In addition, rioters destroyed or looted several convents, mission schools, and parish houses in the district and vandalized or desecrated a great deal of Christian property," reports Bauman.[9] At least four Christians were murdered, thousands were left homeless, and the seeds of terror were sown.

That set the stage for the 2008 Kandhamal Pogrom.

"The 2007 Hindu-Christian riots in Odisha were, at the time, the most damaging and widespread in India's independent history, but they pale in comparison to the violence unleashed on the same region just eight months later," writes Bauman.[10] It began on 23 August 2008 when the VHP leader who figured in the 2007 violence was assassinated. Local communist insurgents claimed credit, and the police also blamed them, but Hindu nationalist outfits seized on the opportunity to — without evidence — blame the Christian community as an excuse to launch an all out assault.

Odisha's VHP state secretary immediately announced, "Christians have killed Swamiji. We will give a befitting reply." Various Sangh groups called for a state-wide shutdown. They planned a public funeral procession of the murdered swami's body — "a meandering, slow-moving, circuitous, 170-kilometer route that was twice as long as necessary and required two days of travel... over undeveloped roads and through many small villages that were still tense from the December violence."[11]

The national VHP chief, Praveen Togadia, traveled to Odisha to join the procession. In his first public remarks upon arriving in the state, he reportedly declared: "A conspiracy has been hatched since long to kill... and the entire Christian community has a hand in it." As Bauman notes, Togadia was "so well known in Odisha" for his "fiery anti-minority rhetoric" that he "had been banned from entering the state during at least one previous period of communal tension and would be banned again later."[12] Nevertheless, Indian human rights activist Harsh Mander reports that the VHP leader "had a free passage across the state in the build-up to the protracted violence," which he used to proclaim: "There is no place for Christians. If Christians don't become Hindus, they have to go. We don't care where they go. They must leave."[13]

"Not surprisingly, as the procession passed slowly through village after village, mourners vented their anger by attacking Christian homes and institutions, sometimes in the presence of police and state government officials," writes Bauman.[14] Indian journalist Prafulla Das reported, "The policemen on duty at various police stations made no attempt to prevent the protesters from attacking Christians and their property. The fact that the police did not open fire anywhere in Kandhamal district to stop the dance of death gave rise to the suspicion that they were acting on the instructions of their political bosses."[15] In at least one case, a local BJP state legislator led the murderous mobs.

The impunity enjoyed by the attackers and the level of police complicity was nowhere more obvious than in the account of a Catholic nun who survived the pogrom. She describes the ordeal, which first began when she and a priest were discovered after seeking refuge in a Hindu man's home:

"The mob entered the room where I was staying in that house. One of them slapped me on my face, caught my hair and pulled me out of the house. Two of them were holding my neck to cut off my head with axe. Others told them to take me out to the road. I saw Father Chellan also being taken out and being beaten.

"The mob, consisting of 40-50 men, was armed with lathis, axes, spades, crowbars, iron rods, sickles, etc. They took both of us to the main road. Then they led us to the burnt down... building, saying that they were going to throw us into the smoldering fire.

"When we reached the... building, they threw me to the verandah, on the way to the dining room, which was full of ashes and broken glass pieces. One of them tore my blouse and others my undergarments. Father Chellan protested and they beat him and pulled him out from there. They pulled out my sari and one of them stepped on my right hand and another on my left hand and then a third person raped me on the verandah.... Then another young man caught me and took me to a room near the staircase. He opened his pants and was attempting to rape me....

"I hid myself under the staircase. The crowd was shouting, 'Where is that sister? Come, let us rape her. At least 100 people should rape.' They found me under the staircase and took me out to the road. There I saw Father Chellan was kneeling down and the crowd was beating him. They were searching for a rope to tie us both together to burn us in the fire. Someone suggested to make us parade naked. They made us to walk on the road....

"When I reached the marketplace, about a dozen of [Odisha] State Armed Police policemen were there. I went to them, asking to protect me, and I sat between two policemen, but they did not move.... The mob said they will come back after eating and one of them who attacked me remained at the police outpost. Policemen then came to the police outpost. They were talking very friendly with the man who had attacked me and stayed back. In police outpost we remained until the inspector in-charge... with his police team came and took us to the station.... The inspector in-charge and other government officers took me privately and asked whatever happened to me. I narrated everything in detail to the police, how I was attacked, raped, taken away from policemen, paraded half-naked, and how the policemen did not help me when I asked for help while weeping bitterly."

When police finally took her away from her attackers, the surviving nun reports that they pressured her not to file charges. When she insisted on doing so, and began writing out her statement, she was urged to "hurry up" and "make it short." She concluded:

"State Police failed to stop the crimes, failed to protect me from the attackers, they were friendly with the attackers, they tried their best that I did not register [charges], not make complaints against police, the police did not take down my statement as I narrated in detail, and they abandoned me half of the way."[16]

For at least a week, mobs burned, massacred, and spread unchecked carnage against Christians — and, in some cases, even Hindus accused of associating with them — throughout the district. "Attacks on houses were often patient and plodding in the same way, suggesting that many of the perpetrators did not fear getting caught," writes Bauman. "The beatings, rapes, killings, dismemberments, and vandalism often, according to victims' testimonies, occurred in an atmosphere of carnival and revelry."

Echoing the ideology of the RSS, the attacking mobs (as reported many survivors) frequently chanted slogans like: "Get rid of the foreign religion; create a Hindu nation."[17]

Violence continued well into September 2008 and, at lower intensity, for months thereafter. By the end of it all, the violence had spread to 600 villages. It was so widespread that accounts of the total damage vary, but perhaps 6,000 homes were burned and looted, 300 to 400 churches were vandalized or totally destroyed, schools and even an orphanage were torched; over 50,000 were left homeless and tens of thousands were relegated to relief camps; nearly 20,000 were injured, and possibly dozens of women gang-raped; and nearly 40 (according to official statistics) lay dead, while some sources estimate that 100 or more were killed.

Meanwhile, thousands of Christians were forced to "re-convert" to Hinduism under threat of death. One victim recounted how her attackers told her: "If you go on being Christians, we will burn your houses and your children in front of you, so make up your minds quickly." Another victim, a pastor who was forced to convert, told a similar story. "If you don't become Hindu, we'll burn your houses too and start killing you," his attackers threatened him.[18]

Everyone knew that the Sangh was responsible for provoking the violence to such heights that it became a pogrom. The National Commission for Minorities, an Indian government entity, primarily blamed the Bajrang Dal. Soon after the violence subsided, Odisha's ruling party severed its alliance with the BJP. The state's chief minister, in 2009, admitted, "Members of RSS, VHP and Bajrang Dal were involved in the violence that took place last year."[19] Out of over 3,000 complaints filed, over 500 of those accused were members of either the RSS, the VHP, or the Bajrang Dal. Yet little justice was ever dealt.

Charges were filed in less than 25 percent of complaints. Many charges were dropped. By the 10th anniversary of the pogrom, in 2018, only 78 people had been convicted. According to one Indian human rights coalition, in 2020, the conviction rate for those charged was barely five percent while, if taken according to the number of complaints filed, it was only one percent.[20]

The 2008 Kandhamal Pogrom was the last major attack on Christians by the RSS-BJP and its supporters prior to the rise of the Modi era in 2014.

Clearly, persecution of Indian Christians is not an entirely new phenomenon. Neither is impunity for their attackers. Neither is police complicity.

"What is different is the intensity, the level, the gravity, the depth of State impunity," says Dayal. What is different is that persecution has become systemic and also systematic. What is different is the geographical extent of the attacks, which are no longer generally isolated to a single region but occur across wide swathes of the country either within short spans of time or simultaneously. What is different is that, while large mobs attack Christians on the streets, BJP officials boldly and openly sit alongside and applaud Hindu nationalist demagogues who calmly call for their slaughter.

"I will not say that Christians are being massacred seven days a week," explains Dayal. "But they can be at a moment's notice."[21]

Such concerns grow increasingly valid considering not only that the RSS's founding fathers denounced Indian Christians as "traitors," and not only the RSS-BJP's history of attacking the community, but especially also the very recent spread of overtly genocidal calls which have accompanied the rise of anti-Christian violence in what many know as Modi's "New India."

Citations:

[1] Narula. "Politics."

[2] "Australia-born missionary, children, burnt alive in Orissa." *Rediff.* 23 January 1999.

[3] Goldenberg, Suzanne. "Bow-and-arrow killer becomes India's most wanted man." *The Guardian.* 27 September 1999.

[4] Bauman, Chad. *Anti-Christian Violence in India.* Ithaca: Cornell University Press. 2020. 147.

[5] Stanley, Alessandra. "Pope Arrives in India Amid Wave of Anti-Christian Sentiment." *The New York Times.* 6 November 1999.

[6] Ganguly, Meenakshi. "Does RSS have any moral standards?" Human Rights Watch. 12 July 2005.

[7] "In photos: Damaged churches, broken homes are the lingering scars of the 2008 Kandhamal riots." *Scroll*. 5 September 2018.

[8] Bauman. 153.

[9] Ibid. 156.

[10] Ibid. 157.

[11] Ibid. 157-158.

[12] Ibid. 158.

[13] Mander, Harsh. "Barefoot: Remembering Kandhamal." *The Hindu*. 17 December 2011.

[14] Bauman. 159.

[15] Das, Prafulla. "Project Orissa." *Frontline*. 26 September 2008.

[16] "Press Statement of Kandhamal Nun, Sister Meena." World Evangelical Alliance. 25 October 2008.

[17] Bauman. 170.

[18] Chamberlain, Gethin. "Convert or we will kill you, Hindu lynch mobs tell fleeing Christians." *The Guardian*. 18 October 2008.

[19] "'Sangh parivar activists involved in Kandhamal riot'." *Zee News*. 24 November 2009.

[20] Apoorvanand. "On the Anniversary of Kandhamal Violence, the Least We Can Do Is Remember." *The Wire*. 25 August 2020.

[21] Dayal. Interview.

5

"Behead Them": The Modi Era's Drive to "Wipe Out" Indian Christians

"In our villages, people keep hand-axes," trumpeted a swami from the stage as over 1,000 people rallied in October 2021 in Chhattisgarh to protest religious conversion. "Why do they keep axes? Behead them — those who come for conversion. Now you'll say that I am spreading hate although I'm a saint. But it's important to ignite the fire sometimes."

Not only should his listeners behead anyone who attempted to convert them, but they should also target those Christians who had already converted. "I want you to talk to them politely first," he said. After that, the policy should be to "stop, warn, and kill." As he ranted, he was cheered on by several BJP "bigwigs" sitting on the stage beside him, including a current Member of Parliament.[1]

As dozens of such anti-conversion rallies were reportedly organized throughout Chhattisgarh in 2021, it is no surprise that the state witnessed the second-highest number of attacks on Christians that year. "In some villages, Christian churches have been vandalized, in others pastors have been beaten or abused," reported *The Guardian*. "Congregations have been broken up by mobs and believers hospitalized with injuries. The police, too, stand accused — of making threats to Christians, hauling them into police stations, and carrying out raids on Sunday prayer services."[2]

In one of the most shocking recent incidents, in October 2021, a mob of 500 led by a local RSS affiliate descended on a group of about 60 Christians who had gathered for a worship service and dinner. Police arrived but reportedly "only observed the ordeal" as the mob rounded up the Christians, searched them, beat several of them, and began pelting them with stones. When police finally intervened, they herded the victims into a bus, detained them for hours at the station, and arrested the host of the gathering on allegations of engaging in "forcible" conversions.[3]

The following month, a mob of 50 besieged 14 Christian homes in a rural village. Invading the houses, they beat men, women, and children, reportedly leaving nine with severe injuries, including broken bones and head wounds. The attackers reportedly declared their intention to make it a "Christian-free" village. A pastor who survived the attack said, "There has been intense opposition in the village against people practicing Christianity. These Christians have been threatened a number of times in the past. Last year, three families fled the village after they were attacked by the right-wing groups. They have never returned to the village."[4]

"Religious conversion is the biggest problem in Chhattisgarh and the top of our agenda," claims the leader of the state's Bajrang Dal unit. He declares: "Bajrang Dal was established for dealing with things in an aggressive manner. Whoever attempts to convert Hindus should be in fear of Bajrang Dal. Bajrang Dal was created for this very purpose." A former BJP chief minister of the state calls conversion a "threat to law and order," claims that those who convert "will also be turned against India," and warns, "Their patriotism then comes under question." A top BJP official says that state party workers have been ordered to make lists of Christians they believe are involved in conversions, surveil them, and work to "fill the jails" with them. "When our party workers are aggressive, then no one can save these pastors," he threatens.

The party workers have indeed grown so aggressive that in one case, a pastor reports that local BJP leaders showed up outside his church to tell him that, if he didn't leave, he would suffer the same fate as Graham Staines.[5]

In December 2021, two months after the anti-conversion rally in Chhattisgarh where the swami demanded that proselytizing Christians be beheaded, similar genocidal calls were raised in Uttar Pradesh (the state with the highest number of attacks on Christians). "Islam should be wiped off this earth," thundered a Hindu nationalist demagogue to a packed conference hall. "Christians also should be wiped off this earth." Arguing that, "if there is any danger" in India then it comes from mosques and churches, he declared, "Islam is a fast poison and Christianity is a slow poison."[6]

These calls to eradicate India's religious minorities are not just echoing in the outskirts of the country. That same month, in Delhi itself, a long-time RSS member and owner of a prominent right-wing TV channel led a crowd of hundreds in a pledge. Their arms raised in a Nazi-style salute, they chanted: "We take an oath and make a resolution that, till our last breath, we will fight, die for and, if need be, kill, to make this country a Hindu nation and keep this country a Hindu nation." Those joining the pledge from the stage included a BJP state minister from the Uttar Pradesh government.[7]

Indian Muslims have long faced the brunt of Hindu nationalist violence, both before and during the Modi era. Tracing all the way back to 1947, they have endured multiple Sangh-led pogroms, including ones which claimed thousands of lives in 1992 and in 2002. Modi himself was implicated in the latter pogrom; an atrocity which led to him being banned from entering the US until his election as prime minister granted him diplomatic immunity. Under his premiership, attacks on Muslims have increasingly escalated. There are countless incidents, many caught on video by the attackers themselves, of Muslims being beaten or even lynched for everything from allegedly possessing beef to keeping company with Hindu girls to praying to simply attempting to engage in commerce. In many cases, Muslims are stopped in the streets by mobs which order them to chant Hindu slogans — in most cases, even if they comply, they are still beaten.

Ideologically, however, Muslims and Christians are both viewed by the Hindu nationalist movement as "foreign" to India. "The first victims of the Modi era were Muslims," reported *The New York Times*. "Then attacks against Christians started ticking up."[8]

Now, as the Modi regime sits unshakably ensconced in the midst of its second term, it appears that the Sangh feels comfortable enough to expand its focus of hatred to include the Christian community. "After seven years of attacks on Muslims, the RSS has now added a new enemy to the lexicon of grievance: Christians," writes Indian journalist Swati Chaturvedi. Christians are joining Muslims, she notes, as "the target of the majoritarian mob baying for the creation of a Hindu Rashtra (exclusivist theocratic Hindu nation) dreamt up by the RSS to replace constitutional democracy in India."[9] As the head of the Chhattisgarh Christian Forum warns: "They want to spread hatred against Christians, as they have done against Muslims."[10]

The scope of the threat as well as the brazenness of the

attackers was perhaps most vividly illustrated in a wave of attacks that occurred throughout multiple states during the 2021 Christmas season. As *The Guardian* reported in December 2021, "In recent years, Christians have increasingly faced harassment around Christmas but this year saw a notable surge in attacks."[11]

In mid-December, a group of Christians in Karnataka was going door-to-door, handing out literature, when a gang attacked them, seized the literature, and burned it in the streets. Police refused to take any action, instead responding, "We have warned the Christian community to not create any communal disharmony by going door-to-door and preaching."[12] Around the same time, elsewhere in the state, a lone attacker armed with a machete entered a Catholic church and chased the priest out into the streets.[13] A few days earlier, in the middle of the day, a mob of 500 invaded a large Catholic school in Madhya Pradesh during classes, shrieking Hindu slogans as they stoned the building's glass exterior.[14]

In one of the most tragically comical incidents, on Christmas Eve, a group of Sangh activists burned an effigy of Santa Claus in Uttar Pradesh. "Santa does not come bearing any gifts," explained the activists. "His only goal is to convert the Hindus to Christianity. It's not going to work anymore. Any attempt at conversion will not be allowed to succeed." Less amusing was when a large group, also in Uttar Pradesh, protested outside the venue of a Christmas Eve service, chanting, "Death to the church." Elsewhere, a church in the northern state of Haryana was hosting a Christmas festival when a gang — some masked — rushed the stage, seized the microphone, demanded to know why the congregation was not celebrating Hindu holidays, and forced them to disperse. Similar disruptions occurred at other churches.[15]

One incident that seized particular attention was the smashing, on Christmas night, of a statue of Jesus standing outside a 19th-century church in Haryana. Security camera footage showed two young men, making no attempt to conceal their identity — and, in fact, filming themselves — as they meticulously spent over an hour tearing down Christmas lights and other decorations before destroying the statue. They clearly feared no repercussions.

"Christmas this year turned out to be very violent," said Pastor Akshay Kumar after his own church in Karnataka was invaded during services. Several of his congregants were wounded, and his wife suffered burns and a fractured knee. "I have been serving as a pastor in this place for the past 20 years and have never faced such aggression." At another church in the state, a mob showed up at a Christmas Eve service, joined by the police, and ordered the congregation to stop the service. Noting that this is the first time his church has ever been forced to cancel services, Pastor Peter said, "We are being hounded by the anti-Christians. The goal is to wipe out Christianity from the village."[16]

In the words of Father Anand, a priest at yet another one of the targeted venues, "These people have impunity, and it creates tension. Every Sunday is a day of terror and trauma for Christians, especially those belonging to those small churches."[17]

Yet it is not only small churches which are under threat nor is it only churches in rural areas.

In November 2021, in a suburb of Delhi, a congregation had gathered for the inaugural service of a warehouse recently converted into a church. During the service, a mob of over a hundred Bajrang Dal activists assembled outside and began vandalizing the building. "India is ours," they chanted. "Shoot the traitor bastards." As one of the attackers filmed the mob, he claimed, speaking to the camera, that it was "an illegally constructed church... where they forcibly converted Hindus." In the video, police can be seen standing by the door of the church as the congregation exits the building, apparently pressured to disperse. As one congregant walks by, someone from the mob shouts out, "Catch that pastor."[18]

"Nothing serious has taken place," a top police official told media regarding the attack. "The church people are making a big issue out of the whole situation."[19] Why, he seemed to be asking, should this group of Christians be concerned about their service being broken up by a violent mob that called them traitors who ought to be shot.

Smaller churches in rural areas, however, also face similar — and sometimes far more invasive — mob assaults. In the northern state of Uttarakhand, in October 2021, a mob of 200, armed with iron rods, barged into a church service where only about a dozen worshippers were present. "The prayer was about to begin. Around ten people were present when the crowd, many of whom we recognized as members of Bajrang Dal and other right-wing groups stormed the church and started beating us and damaging the church property," reported one of the church leaders.[20] Attackers destroyed everything. Congregants were dragged from the church, several were injured, and one was hospitalized.

Three months later, only two arrests had been made — one of a VHP leader, another of a BJP activist. Multiple other local BJP workers, though named by the victims, remained at-large.

The assault, which occurred on 3 October, was

especially notable in that it was one of at least 13 separate attacks on Christians in a single day across five states plus Delhi.[21] Most of them were by mobs busting up services, usually beating the congregants and severely vandalizing the churches. In most cases, police arrested the victims. In Delhi, a gang of a dozen men reportedly invaded a pastor's home and threatened him to stop preaching.

As repeatedly highlighted, not only are police throughout India generally reluctant to take any real action against attackers but they are often more likely to arrest the victims. Beyond that, however, in some places, the deeper state apparatus is being actively turned against Christians.

In October 2021, Indian media outlet *The Quint* discovered evidence that the BJP-ruled state government of Karnataka had issued a series of orders to, essentially, spy on churches. The State Intelligence Department, it emerged, had been tasked with "a massive intelligence gathering exercise" focused on identifying the locations of all churches and identities of their leadership. "Viewed in its totality, the intelligence wing has aimed to identify people who practice or preach Christianity in all places of their worship — from established churches that have stood for centuries, to newer churches of younger Christian denominations, and even homes were community prayer gatherings are held," reported *Quint*.[22]

Shortly after, the outlet discovered that some in the state were going even a step further, issuing orders for tax officials to conduct door-to-door surveys to identify and document any and all "Hindus who have converted to Christianity."[23]

Responding to the news, Metropolitan Archbishop of Bengaluru (the capital of Karnataka) Peter Machado stated, "What the government seems to be saying is that you can be a Christian, but be a Christian only in your conscience. They seem to be saying, don't declare it (Christian faith), wear it or show it. I don't think this is possible. India is a free country."[24]

Not only at the state but also at the national level, however, the RSS-BJP combine seem intent on doing whatever they can to ensure that India will no longer be a free country for Christians.

Most notably, the national government has stripped countless religious charities of the right to receive foreign funding, forcing many to shutter their operations within the country. One of the largest groups targeted was Compassion International, a Christian humanitarian aid organization known especially for their child-sponsorship program. The organization, which had operated in India since 1968, was supporting a network of nearly 600 Indian Christian charities and sponsoring almost 150,000 children when its foreign contributions license was revoked in 2017. The explanation? They were engaging in "activities against the national interest."

"We do believe that Compassion and other Christian charities are being singled out because of our faith, and that the Indian government is trying to limit the expansion of Christianity in India," said the organization's spokesperson at the time.[25]

"Adverse inputs" was the reason given on Christmas Day 2021 for the government's refusal to renew the foreign contributions license of Missionaries of Charity, the organization founded by Mother Teresa in 1950 to, in particular, rescue abandoned street children and provide care homes for terminally-ill people from impoverished backgrounds. "Government agencies have given a cruel Christmas gift to the poorest of the poor," said Fr. Dominic

Gomes, Vicar General of the Archdiocese of Calcutta, the region where Mother Teresa first began her efforts. Denouncing the "timing and lack of empathy," he declared, "This latest attack on the Christian Community and their social outreach is even more a dastardly attack on the poorest of India's poor."[26]

Two weeks later, and only after the news provoked outrage in media around the world, the government relented and renewed the license.

Meanwhile, the specter of a national anti-conversion law continues to haunt the psyches of Indian Christians, especially as such laws are passed with increasing frequency in BJP-ruled state after BJP-ruled state. With the Modi government due to remain in power until 2022, and as it faces no tangible opposition whatsoever, that possibility seems more like a probability. Moreover, many in the cult of Modi would be delighted to see him retain the premiership indefinitely. And — whether via government legislation or mob violence — the drive to "wipe out" Indian Christians appears likely to continue unabated.

That drive was further advanced, in January 2022, when, in one of the most explicit echoes of the old-guard RSS leadership's description of Indian Christians — and Muslims — as "traitors," a conclave of Hindu nationalists gathered in Uttarakhand to, among other things, demand that religious conversion be placed in the category of "treason" and punished by the death penalty.[27]

Citations:

[1] Jafri, Alishan. "Hate Watch: In Presence of BJP Bigwigs, Chhattisgarh Hindutva Leader Calls for Beheading Minorities." *The Wire.* 21 October 2021.

2 Ellis-Petersen, Hannah. "India's Christians living in fear as claims of 'forced conversions' swirl." *The Guardian*. 3 October 2021.

3 "Hindu Nationalist Mob Holds Christians against their Will." *Morning Star News*. 3 November 2021.

4 "Radical Hindu Nationalists Brutally Attack Christian Community in India." International Christian Concern. 8 November 2021.

5 Ellis-Petersen. "Fear."

6 HindutvaWatch. Twitter Post. 31 December. 2021. https://twitter.com/HindutvaWatchIn/status/1476913579466969091

7 "In Delhi, Hindutva Groups Vow To 'Fight, Die & Kill' To Make India Hindu Rashtra." *The Quint*. 23 December 2021.

8 Gettleman and Raj. "Persecution."

9 Chaturvedi, Swati. "Modi's Politics of Hate Come for India's Christians, Amid Calls to Kill Muslims." *Haaretz*. 29 December 2021.

10 Aswani, Tarushi. "At Raipur Dharma Sansad, Hindutva Leaders Raise Call to Take Up Arms for Hindu Rashtra." *The Wire*. 30 December 2021.

11 Ellis-Petersen, Hannah. "Jesus statue smashed in spate of attacks on India's Christian community." *The Guardian*. 27 December 2021.

12 MS, Sreeja. "In Karnataka, Right-Wing Groups Set Christian Religious Books On Fire." *NDTV*. 12 December 2021.

13 "Man threatens priest with machete in Belagavi church." *The Times of India*. 12 December 2021.

14 Jain, Ayesha and Vishnukant Tiwari. "Right-Wing Mob Vandalises Missionary School in MP, Alleges Religious Conversion." *The Quint*. 7 December 2021.

15 Barton, Naomi. "Hindutva Brigade Disrupts 7 Christmas Events Across India." *The Wire*. 26 December 2021.

16 "Christians in India's Karnataka State Endure a Violent Christmas." International Christian Concern. 14 January 2022.

17 Ellis-Petersen. "Statue."

18 HindutvaWatch. Twitter Post. 29 November 2021. https://twitter.com/HindutvaWatchIn/status/1465572475878608896

19 Jain, Nikita. "Tensions High in Dwarka After Right-Wing Hindu Mob Vandalises Church." *The Wire*. 30 November 2021.

20 Susheel, Tapan. "Uttarakhand: Mob vandalises church in Roorkee; 5 hurt." *The Times of India*. 4 October 2021.

21 "13 attacks on Christians in one day; Religious freedom in danger in North India – Report." *Morning Express*. 16 October 2021.

22 Henry, Nikhila. "Not Just a 'Survey': Karnataka Govt Gets Intelligence Wing to Spy on Churches." *The Quint*. 23 October 2021.

23 Henry, Nikhila. "Another Dubious Church 'Survey': Karnataka BJP Govt Tracing 'Christian Converts'." *The Quint*. 29 November 2021.

24 Henry, Nikhila. "Why Target Christians? Bengaluru Archbishop on Dubious Karnataka Church 'Survey'." *The Quint*. 24 October 2021.

25 Bhalla, Nita. "India's NGO crackdown forces U.S. Christian charity out after half a century." *Reuters*. 14 March 2017.

26 "Missionaries of Charity Says FCRA Renewal Not Approved by MHA, But 'No Freeze Ordered'." *The Wire*. 27 December 2021.

27 "Seers at Mela want India to be declared a Hindu nation." *The Times of India*. 30 January 2022.

6

Desperate Plight of Indian Christians Demands a Global Outcry

Whatever Modi's political future, the RSS-BJP combine has held such an iron-clad grip on national (and much state) power for so long, and with so little resistance (internally or internationally), that it and its affiliated cadres have managed to sow the seeds of hate so far, so wide, and so deep that India will, inevitably, be reaping a harvest of hate for generations to come. Masses of the population, ranging from the ancient to the new-born, have been and will continue to be — barring some miracle — propagandized, brainwashed, and radicalized to think about and act towards their fellow citizens with the most venomous hatred imaginable. Mass violence seems inevitable.

Whenever the Modi era comes to an end, it seems likely that whoever replaces him may well be someone even more overtly radical and supportive of the extremist forces that are now dominating the streets of India. That's a cause for global concern.

India currently contains the second-largest population in the world — nearly one in five people on the planet. Its Christian and Muslim populations combined constitute approximately 300 million people, a population size ranking in the top five most-populated countries in the world. India is not only the world's largest democracy but also the only historically *stable and secular* democracy in South Asia. Until 2014, in many ways, the Republic of

India had great potential to be the regional bastion of freedom, thoroughly pluralist society, welcome ally of all other truly democratic nations, and economic power-house that could have secured it a well-deserved place of global leadership. Now, however, as the RSS-BJP regime oversees the country's transition into a breeding ground for religious extremists hell-bent on eradicating minorities, India is swiftly becoming a threat not only to regional but also global stability.

Indian Muslims, in the Modi era, have already suffered to such a great degree that international experts are warning they are at risk of genocide. In January 2022, for instance, Dr. Gregory Stanton of Genocide Watch explained, "Genocide is not an event. It is a process. It develops." Thus, noting that many of the various "stages of genocide" — "which are not linear; they occur simultaneously" — are currently present in modern India, he warned:

> "We believe there is a real risk of massacres. What is, of course, extremely troubling here is that the Modi government has stood back, said nothing, and will be very happy to just watch it happen. That is exactly what Modi did in Gujarat in 2002. It is what he will do again. So, this massacre — this genocide — will likely not be even carried out by the Indian State. It will likely be carried out by mobs.... We believe that India is at the Persecution Stage right now. That's the stage right before genocide."[1]

If that's the potential situation facing Indian Muslims, who make up approximately 14 percent of the population, then what fate may await Indian Christians, who constitute barely three percent?

As Indian Christians are, more and more often, falling within the crosshairs of hate, there are already some indications that the Church, in various areas of India, is being driven underground. "Pastors hold clandestine ceremonies at night," reported *The New York Times* in December 2021. "They conduct secret baptisms. They pass out audio Bibles that look like little transistor radios so that illiterate farmers can surreptitiously listen to the scripture as they plow their fields." The paper profiled one such pastor who has gone covert:

"Vinod Patil, a Pentecostal preacher in Madhya Pradesh, is not giving up. Just as Hindu extremists believe it is their duty to stop conversions out of Hinduism, Pastor Patil believes his religious duty is to spread Christianity. These days, he operates like a secret agent.

"He leaves his house quietly and never in a group. He jumps on a small Honda motorbike and putters past little towns and scratchy wheat fields, Bible tucked inside his jacket. He constantly checks his mirrors to make sure he is not tailed.

"Hindu extremists have warned Pastor Patil that they will kill him if they catch him preaching. So last year he shut down his Living Hope Pentecostal Church, which he said used to have 400 members, and shifted to small clandestine services, usually at night.

"He knows the vigilantes are looking for him. But he insists that he is following the law and that everyone who comes to his meetings does so voluntarily.

"'Before, when we had a problem, we'd go to

the police,' he said. 'Now, the anti-Christians have the government with them. The anti-Christians are everywhere.'"[2]

The trend of persecution held steady as a new year dawned upon India. "The attacks on [the] Christian community continue in the year 2022 as nothing is being done by the people in power to control it," reported AC Michael of the United Christian Forum on 26 January 2022. "In just 25 days of this year, 31 incidents of violence against Christians [have occurred] in nine states of India with Chhattisgarh leading the chart with eight incidents."[3]

Without action by the people in power, the year 2022 will likely follow the exact same pattern as the previous seven years of the Modi era: an uptick in anti-Christian attacks. If there were 505 documented attacks in 2021, how many will occur in 2022? There is no logical reason to expect anything else except more — and more vicious — attacks this year than there were last year.

Despite such a high number of incidents, the figures must be properly contextualized to avoid underestimating the true impact on the Indian Christian community. For one thing, 505 attacks in 2021 represents only *documented* incidents; a great many more may have gone unreported. For another thing, it's crucial to remember that the majority of documented attacks were *mob attacks* by, at times, hundreds of people. Most attacks were not against individuals, but rather entire congregations of dozens, scores, or more, meaning that thousands of people may have been directly victimized. Moreover, such attacks — especially considering how they usually involve impunity for the attackers and arrests of the victims — spread *psychological terror* which almost certainly impacts tens and tens of thousands, if not millions, of Indian Christians.

Solutions to the current scenario are not easily found. It is difficult to believe, according to a realistic evaluation of the facts at hand, that the situation will get better before it gets far worse. The gravity of the plight of Indian Christians — and Muslims — is that many may well end up being sent to their graves before they begin to see the rising tide of oppression recede. In some ways, however, the apparent hopelessness of the situation may, in and of itself, offer a glimmer of hope *if it can capture the attention of the international community.*

India's religious minorities, whether Christian or Muslim, are in no position whatsoever to resist the oppression they face. Doing so, *even peacefully*, does little but place them at greater risk. The mere fact of their existence, after all, poses an "internal threat" to the nation by those viewed as "traitors" in the eyes of the RSS-BJP. Meanwhile, the political opposition to the BJP is in total disarray. Not only is it virtually non-existent, but the Modi regime has increasingly targeted its critics from the opposition (in political, social, and journalistic circles), in some cases even jailing many of them on framed conspiracy charges.

True, effective, and lasting change in India can only come from within the country, but how and when it will come is beyond the imagination. Until that time, however, a modicum of reprieve for the persecuted religious minorities of India may come via international pressure. Such pressure might, additionally, influence even a BJP-ruled India to at least attempt to rein in the ruthless forces that have been unleashed on the streets.

For the past several years, there has been a growing but still scattered collection of voices, rising from within the free democracies of the world, which recognize and denounce the expanding atrocities of the Modi regime. These include a large number of human rights organizations and, less commonly, national-level politicians. In the case of persecution of Indian Muslims, many Islamic groups around the world are also, finally, starting to perk up and speak out.

Yet practically no one is standing up for the persecuted Christians of India — least of all the international Church. In fact, especially in the West, the Church is not only largely, if not completely, silent about the oppression of her brothers and sisters in India but actually appears to be totally ignorant that there is even any issue at all.

One of the few American Christian clergy who is aware of — and talking about — the issue is Father Joshua Lickter, an Anglican priest in California who agrees about the general ignorance of the international Church regarding Indian Christian persecution. "They don't know what's happening," says Fr. Lickter about Christians outside India. He believes it's imperative, however, that they *must* know, stating: "We have a duty as Christians to speak out against this rising persecution. We need to play our part to help set the oppressed free. If we don't raise our voices, persecution will only continue to increase. The Christians in India need us to speak out."[4]

What can be done to alleviate the suffering of Christians in India today? At the very least, their fellow Christians around the globe can, considering it their moral obligation, learn of the sad plight of their brothers and sisters in India. They can educate themselves first, and then — their minds fully informed — they can follow the lead of their consciences which will, undoubtedly, compel them to begin speaking out.

India today is at a crossroads. Will it pass over into totalitarian rule, completely subjected to the fascistic forces of a genocidal movement which is dedicated to making India a theocratic State? Or will it reverse course and not only return to, but expand upon, its original foundation as a free democracy committed to upholding, preserving, and celebrating the equal rights of all?

The outcome of the Hindu nationalist efforts to eradicate Christianity in the country will certainly play a central role in determining India's future course.

Citations:

[1] Justice for All. "Save India From Fascism - Gregory Stanton." *YouTube*. 17 January 2022. https://youtu.be/WHpLcSWxIHU

[2] Gettleman and Raj. "Persecution."

[3] Michael, AC. Twitter Post. 26 January 2022. https://twitter.com/ACMichael1/status/1486580031723741192

[4] Lickter, Fr. Joshua. Personal interviews. January 2022.

— Glossary —

Anti-conversion law: Laws in India which criminalize religious conversion without first informing or, often, receiving permission from the local government. Nine states currently enforce them; several others are either in process of passing them or considering them. The majority were either passed or updated during BJP rule since 2014.

Bajrang Dal: Youth wing of the VHP, founded in 1984.

BJP: Bharatiya Janata Party, the political wing of the RSS, founded in 1980. The BJP has held total national control of India since 2014.

Golwalkar, MS: The 2nd chief of the RSS, who headed it from 1940 to 1973. Known as the RSS's "Guru," he is the paramilitary's longest-serving and most influential leader. He authored two books (1939 and 1966) which offer detailed and unvarnished insight into Hindutva ideology.

Hedgewar, KB: The 1st chief of the RSS, who headed it from 1925 to 1940.

Hindu Nationalism: The prevailing ideology of the Sangh Parivar, which includes India's ruling BJP. Hindu nationalism is usually interchangeable with "Hindutva."

Hindustan: A name for India meaning "land of the Hindus" which has long historical usage but, today, is often used by Hindu nationalist elements to emphasize their believe that India is a Hindu nation.

Hindutva: A term popularized by VD Savarkar, author of a book with the same name, Hindutva is essentially a religious nationalist political ideology which views Hindus as the only residents of India who possess a natural birthright to the land and treats non-Hindus, especially Christians and Muslims, as either second-class citizens or outright "foreign elements." The term can be viewed as generally synonymous with Hindu nationalism.

Modi, Narendra: A lifelong RSS member, BJP politician, and Prime Minister of India since 2014.

Moonje, BS: A co-founder of the RSS, Hedgewar's mentor, and the man who visited the European fascists and wanted to model the RSS after them.

RSS: Rashtriya Swayamsevak Sangh, a paramilitary and the original Hindu nationalist organization in the Sangh Parivar, founded in 1925. The RSS is the fountainhead of "Hindutva" and the incubator for many BJP politicians, including Prime Minister Narendra Modi. It has been banned three times since 1947.

Sangh Parivar: Meaning "Family of Organizations," Sangh Parivar is an umbrella term for the RSS and the groups springing from it. It is often shortened to simply "the Sangh."

Savarkar, VD: Author of the 1923 book "Hindutva," which popularized use of the term. His brother was a co-founder of the RSS.

VHP: Vishwa Hindu Parishad, the religious wing of the RSS, founded in 1964.

— Acknowledgements —

My gratitude to Hindutva Watch [HindutvaWatch.com], a project for documenting Hindu nationalist atrocities which translated most of the videos referenced in this work. My love and admiration to the Indian Christian community who, as this work hopefully demonstrates just a little bit, so often refuse to bend and bow to the intense pressure — and often violence — they face simply for believing what they believe. My humble plea to Christians, *especially clergy*, around the world to incline their ears to the increasingly desperate situation of their own in India.

— About the Author —

Pieter Friedrich is a freelance journalist specializing in analysis of South Asian affairs. Born in California, he is the author of *Sikh Caucus: Siege in Delhi, Surrender in Washington* (2021) and *Saffron Fascists: India's Hindu Nationalist Rulers* (2020) as well as co-author of *Captivating the Simple-Hearted: A Struggle for Human Dignity in the Indian Subcontinent* (2017). A frequent speaker at universities, seminars, and protests, he engages with issues such as human rights, supremacist political ideologies, ethno-nationalism, politicization of religion, authoritarian government structures and policies, state-sponsored atrocities, and the need to unify around doctrines of liberty and a politics of reconciliation rather than hate.

Printed by Amazon Italia Logistica S.r.l.
Torrazza Piemonte (TO), Italy

46057794R00042